UNMASKING JEZEBEL'S INTERCESSORS OFFICIAL WORKBOOK

CONQUER THE DEMONIC SPIRIT HIJACKING WHAT GOD IS BUILDING IN YOUR LIFE

JENNIFER LECLAIRE

CONTENTS

INTRODUCTION

Welcome to the "Unmasking Jezebel's Intercessors Official Workbook," a comprehensive guide designed to equip you with the knowledge, understanding, and spiritual tools needed to identify, confront, and overcome the influence of the Jezebel spirit in your life, community, and place of worship. This workbook is not merely a collection of teachings; it's a journey into deep spiritual truths aimed at delivering freedom and fostering healing. Through this workbook, you will embark on a transformative path, uncovering the deceptions of one of the most insidious spirits encountered by the church today: the spirit of Jezebel and its intercessors.

The spirit of Jezebel, characterized by manipulation, control, seduction, and intimidation, seeks to undermine the authority and purity of God's people. It's a spirit that has wreaked havoc throughout biblical history and continues to do so in contemporary times. However, this workbook offers more than just an exploration of Jezebel's characteristics; it provides a strategic approach to spiritual warfare, designed to empower you to stand firm against the schemes of the enemy and to walk in victory.

Key Takeaways and Expectations

- **Deep Biblical Insight**: Drawing from both Old and New Testament scriptures, you will gain a comprehensive understanding of the Jezebel spirit's origins, operations, and objectives. This biblical foundation is crucial for recognizing the spirit's influence in your life and community.
- **Discernment and Identification**: Learn to discern the subtle workings of Jezebel's intercessors. This workbook will guide you through the signs and symptoms of Jezebel's influence, helping you to identify not just the overt manifestations but the more deceptive, hidden operations of this spirit.
- **Strategies for Overcoming**: Armed with knowledge, you will be equipped with practical strategies for engaging in effective

spiritual warfare. From cultivating a deep relationship with God to employing the authority given to you as a believer, you will discover how to combat the influence of Jezebel and secure your spiritual freedom.

- **Personal and Community Healing**: Jezebel's influence often leaves wounds that can hinder personal growth and communal harmony. This workbook includes guided reflections and prayers aimed at healing these wounds, restoring relationships, and strengthening the body of Christ.

- **Empowerment to Stand Firm**: As you progress through the workbook, expect to be empowered to stand firm in your identity in Christ. You will be encouraged to exercise your God-given authority to protect yourself, your family, and your community from the advances of the enemy.

- **Enhanced Prayer Life**: Engage in targeted prayer strategies that dismantle Jezebel's strongholds and release God's power and restoration in your life. The workbook emphasizes the importance of intercession, teaching you how to pray effectively against the spirit of Jezebel.

What You Will Receive

This workbook is designed to be interactive, featuring reflective questions, actionable steps, and journaling prompts that facilitate personal introspection and spiritual growth. Each chapter is crafted to build upon the last, creating a layered understanding of spiritual warfare against the Jezebel spirit.

By the end of this workbook, you will not only have a thorough understanding of Jezebel's intercessors but also possess the spiritual resilience to resist and overcome their influence. Whether you are a new believer or a seasoned intercessor, this workbook is a vital resource for anyone committed to living a life of freedom and purity in Christ.

Embrace this journey with an open heart and a willing spirit, ready to dive deep into the truths of God's Word and to apply these lessons to your life. Let the "Unmasking Jezebel's Intercessors Official Workbook" be your guide as you step into the authority and victory that Christ has won for you. Together, let's embark on this journey of unmasking, confronting, and overcoming the spirit of Jezebel, for the glory of God and the advancement of His Kingdom.

HOW TO USE THIS WORKBOOK

"Unmasking Jezebel's Intercessors Official Workbook." This guide is designed to lead you step-by-step into a deeper understanding of confronting and overcoming the Jezebel spirit. To maximize the impact of this workbook in your spiritual walk, it's crucial to approach it with intentionality and commitment. Here are 10 key points to help you effectively utilize this workbook and ensure you receive the full benefits of each chapter.

1. Begin with Prayer

Before diving into each chapter, start with prayer. Invite the Holy Spirit to guide your understanding and to illuminate the truths contained within these pages. Prayer sets the foundation for revelation and prepares your heart to receive what God has for you through this study.

2. Dedicate Time for Study

Set aside dedicated time for study without distractions. This workbook is not meant to be rushed through; it requires thoughtful engagement and reflection. Consistent, uninterrupted time in study allows you to deeply process the information and apply it to your life.

3. Read Each Chapter Thoroughly

Read each chapter thoroughly, including the scriptural references. The insights in this workbook are grounded in biblical truth, and understanding the scriptural context is key to grasping the full extent of Jezebel's tactics and how to combat them.

4. Reflect on the Reflective Questions

After reading each chapter, spend time reflecting on the questions provided. These questions are designed to prompt personal introspection and spiritual assessment. Write down your answers and thoughts in a journal or notebook. This practice can reveal areas of vulnerability to the Jezebel spirit and areas where growth is happening.

5. Engage with the Actionable Steps

Each chapter includes actionable steps that encourage you to put what you've learned into practice. Engage with these steps earnestly, as they are practical tools for building spiritual resilience and authority. Whether it's enhancing your prayer life or cultivating discernment, these actions are vital for applying the knowledge gained.

6. Utilize the Journaling Prompts

The journaling prompts provided in each chapter are there to facilitate deeper spiritual exploration and expression. Use them to document your journey, insights, struggles, and victories. Journaling is a powerful way to track your growth and the ways God speaks to you throughout this study.

7. Study in Community

If possible, go through this workbook with a study group or a spiritual mentor. Discussing the chapters with others can provide additional insights and support. Community study fosters accountability and encourages the sharing of personal experiences and revelations.

8. Implement Regular Review Sessions

Regularly review the key points and lessons from previous chapters. This repetition reinforces the learning and allows the Holy Spirit to reveal new layers of understanding. Revisiting the material can also provide clarity on concepts that were initially challenging.

9. Pray Through the Prayers and Declarations

Each chapter contains specific prayers and declarations. Don't just read them—pray them out loud and with authority. These prayers are crafted to address the issues discussed in the chapters directly, invoking God's power and protection against the influence of the Jezebel spirit.

10. Apply the Lessons to Your Life

Finally, the most critical step is to apply the lessons learned to your life. This workbook is not just about acquiring knowledge; it's about transformation. Take deliberate steps to change your prayer strategies, engage in spiritual warfare, and fortify your walk with God based on the insights you've gained.

This workbook is a tool God can use to bring about significant growth and freedom in your life. Approach each chapter with an open heart, ready to learn and be transformed. May your journey through the "Unmasking Jezebel's Intercessors Official Workbook" lead you into greater victory, deeper understanding, and a more intimate relationship with God.

CHAPTER I

HELLO, MY NAME IS JEZEBEL

This reminder encourages us to stand firm against spiritual threats with faith and courage, knowing we are not alone in our battles.

Joshua 1:9 (NKJV): "Have I not commanded you? Be strong and of good courage; do not be afraid, nor be dismayed, for the Lord your God is with you wherever you go."

I n our journey to unmask Jezebel's intercessors, we begin with an understanding that **Jezebel represents a spiritual threat that does not announce its presence overtly.** This spirit, much like a silent infiltrator, seeks to harm communities, churches, and individuals from the shadows. It's crucial to recognize that the Jezebel spirit operates under the radar, making it a hidden threat that requires discernment to detect. The subtlety of this spirit is its strength, allowing it to cause damage before anyone realizes it has infiltrated their midst.

Drawing from Mick Jagger's "Sympathy for the Devil," I found a poignant analogy. This song, starting from Satan's perspective, offers a unique lens through which we can understand **the deceptive charm of Jezebel**. Just as the song's narrator introduces himself with a veneer of wealth and taste, Jezebel's intercessors often present themselves in an appealing light. They may appear committed, eloquent, and anointed, making them difficult to immediately discern. Their charm and commitment can easily mislead, as their true aim is to sow discord and lead astray.

One of the challenges we face in our communities is **misidentification and false accusations**. It's a delicate balance to maintain. Assertive individuals or those with a passionate heart for God's Kingdom can be wrongfully labeled as Jezebels. This not only harms the accused but also diverts attention from the true Jezebel spirits operating undercover. We must tread carefully, ensuring not to mistake passion for manipulation or assertiveness for control.

To effectively combat this spirit, we must delve into

understanding the true nature of the Jezebel spirit. It's not merely about controlling or manipulative behavior; it's a deeper, more insidious motive of seduction and destruction. The Jezebel spirit seeks to lead people away from their faith, into sin and idolatry. Recognizing the essence of this spirit is vital in developing strategies to confront and overcome it.

The historical and biblical background of Jezebel provides key insights into her modus operandi. From her actions in the scriptures, we learn that **Jezebel's historical and biblical background** is not just a tale of old but a lesson that echoes into our current spiritual battles. Understanding Jezebel's allegiance to the deities Ashtoreth and Baal helps us to grasp the depth of her influence and the spiritual warfare that we are engaged in.

At its core, **the seductive power of Jezebel** is what we must guard against. This spirit uses seduction as its primary weapon, aiming to lead the faithful astray. Our defenses against such tactics must be rooted in prayer, discernment, and a deep commitment to our faith. By recognizing the seductive strategies employed by Jezebel, we can better prepare ourselves for the spiritual battles that lie ahead.

The role of spiritual discernment cannot be overstated. **The importance of spiritual discernment** in identifying and combating the Jezebel spirit is critical.

> *We need the Holy Spirit's guidance to see beyond the surface, to discern the true nature of the threats we face. This discernment allows us to distinguish between genuine spiritual anointing and the deceptive charms that Jezebel's intercessors might display.*

For those called to stand in the gap, **the role of intercessors in combating Jezebel** is a divine mandate. Through prayer and spiritual warfare, intercessors can protect their communities from the influence of the Jezebel spirit. It is a call to vigilance, to prayer, and to the wielding of spiritual authority granted to us through Christ.

As we move forward, **a call to action against Jezebel** is clear. We must not only be aware of this spirit's workings but also actively engage in the spiritual warfare required to defeat it. This involves prayer, discernment, and a steadfast commitment to spiritual integrity. We are called to stand firm in our faith, to resist the seductions of Jezebel, and to protect the purity of our communities.

In closing, I encourage each of you to cultivate a deep

relationship with God, seeking His wisdom and guidance in all things. Equip yourselves with knowledge of the Scriptures and the teachings of the church on spiritual warfare. Engage in prayer and intercession, standing firm against the advances of the Jezebel spirit. Together, through God's grace and our diligence, we can protect our communities and ensure that the seductive allure of Jezebel finds no foothold among us.

REFLECTIVE QUESTIONS

1. Have you ever encountered a situation where you felt a deceptive or manipulative spirit was at work? How did you respond?
2. Reflect on the analogy of "Sympathy for the Devil." How does this comparison deepen your understanding of the subtlety of spiritual threats like Jezebel?
3. Consider the times you may have misjudged someone's assertive personality as a "Jezebel spirit." What impact did that have on your relationship with them?
4. How do you discern the difference between genuine spiritual anointing and deceptive

charm that could be attributed to the Jezebel spirit?

5. What steps can you take to enhance your spiritual discernment to better identify and combat the Jezebel spirit in your community?

Actionable Steps

- **Cultivate a Prayerful Attitude**: Consistently seek guidance and wisdom from the Holy Spirit through prayer, asking for discernment in identifying the true nature of the spirits at work around you.

- **Equip Yourself with Knowledge**: Study the characteristics of the Jezebel spirit as described in the Bible and other reliable spiritual resources. Understanding the historical context and biblical descriptions will enhance your ability to recognize its manifestations.

- **Engage in Spiritual Warfare**: Actively participate in intercessory prayer, specifically against the Jezebel spirit, using the authority given to you through Christ. Engage with a community of believers for support and accountability in this spiritual battle.

. . .

JOURNALING **Prompt**

Reflect on a time when you faced a challenging situation that required discernment to identify underlying spiritual forces. Write about how you felt, how you sought guidance, and what the outcome was. Consider how this experience can inform your approach to spiritual warfare and intercession in the future.

∽

~

_____

_____

_____

_____

_____

_____

_____

_____

_____

_____

_____

_____

_____

_____

_____

_____

_____

_____

_____

_____

_____

_____

_____

_____

_____

~

_____

_____

_____

_____

_____

_____

_____

_____

_____

_____

_____

_____

_____

_____

_____

_____

_____

_____

_____

_____

_____

CHAPTER 2
INTERCESSORS OF LIGHT

As intercessors, our prayers and actions can illuminate paths, leading others to discover the love and grace found in Christ.

"Let your light so shine before men, that they may see your good works and glorify your Father in heaven."- (Matthew 5:16, NKJV)

As we venture into the realm of spiritual warfare and the pivotal role of intercessors, it's essential to grasp the depth and breadth of our calling. The journey of an intercessor is not taken lightly—it is a path illuminated by the **Historical Significance of Lighthouses**, a beacon guiding us through treacherous waters to safety. Just as ancient mariners relied on these lighthouses to navigate perilous seas, we, as intercessors, serve a similar purpose in the spiritual realm. Our prayers and intercessions warn of dangers, guide to safety, and ultimately save lives.

The **Role of Lightkeepers** is a profound analogy for our spiritual duty. These keepers ensured the lighthouse's light never dimmed, much like we are charged with keeping the flame of intercession burning brightly. This continuous vigilance in prayer and dedication to the Word ensures that the light of Christ within us never flickers out, guiding many to the safety of God's presence.

As **Intercessors as Modern-Day Keepers of the Flame**, we are reminded of the importance of our vigil.

The Word of God, likened to a lamp unto our feet, serves as our guide, our source of strength, and the fuel that keeps our flame alive.

Through diligent study and prayer, we combat the darkness, leading souls out of bondage and into the liberating light of Christ.

The calling to be **Intercessors of Light** is a divine commission, setting us apart as warriors in the spiritual domain. This calling is not for the faint-hearted; it requires courage, dedication, and a willingness to venture into darkness armed with the light of God's Word. Our mission is to penetrate the darkest corners of this world, breaking the chains of demonic strongholds and setting captives free.

Our exemplar in this mission is none other than Christ Himself, the **Chief Intercessor**. His life, a testament to the power of intercession, provides us with the blueprint for our prayer lives. Jesus' dedication to prayer, His constant communication with the Father, and His ultimate sacrifice on the cross underscore the profound impact of intercessory prayer.

Understanding what constitutes **True Intercession** is critical in distinguishing ourselves from the false intercessors inspired by the spirit of Jezebel. True intercession is characterized by its purity, alignment with God's will, and its foundation on the truth of God's Word. It is a prayer that seeks not personal gain but the fulfillment of God's kingdom on Earth.

Yet, we must be aware that **Jezebel Hates True Intercession**. This spirit seeks to undermine the work of God's intercessors by promoting falsehood, deception, and discord.

As warriors of light, we must be vigilant,
discerning, and steadfast in our commit-
ment to truth and righteousness.

The **Marks of Intercessors of Light** distinguish us from those who operate in the shadows. Our sacrifice, dedication to God's will, perseverance in prayer, and humility in service are the hallmarks of our ministry. These qualities, inspired by the life and work of Jesus, empower us to stand firm against the wiles of the enemy and to intercede effectively for the kingdom of God.

Living as **The Light of the World** is our ultimate calling as intercessors. In a world often shrouded in darkness, our lives must reflect the light of Christ, guiding others to the truth and hope found in Him. Our prayers, our actions, and our very beings should serve as beacons of hope, leading the lost to the safe harbor of God's love.

As we **Pray in the Light**, let us remember the privilege and responsibility of our calling. Our prayers have the power to break chains, to illuminate darkness, and to usher in the kingdom of God. Let us then approach this calling with reverence, humility, and a steadfast heart, fully committed to being intercessors of light in a world desperate for the truth and love of Christ.

REFLECTIVE QUESTIONS

1. How do you see yourself as a modern-day keeper of the flame, and in what ways do you maintain your spiritual light?
2. Reflect on a time when you felt called to intercede in a dark situation. How did you respond, and what was the outcome?
3. Considering Christ's example as the Chief Intercessor, how can you model your intercessory prayers after Him?
4. In what ways can you differentiate between true and false intercession, especially in environments influenced by the spirit of Jezebel?
5. What personal steps can you take to ensure you are walking as a child of light, especially in challenging times?

Actionable Steps

- **Cultivate a Relationship with the Word:** Immerse yourself in Scripture daily. It fuels your intercession, enlightens your path, and strengthens your resolve against darkness.
- **Equip Yourself with Discernment:** Pray for the gift of discernment to recognize the difference between true and false intercession

and to understand the specific needs of those you are called to pray for.

- **Engage in Strategic Intercession**: Actively seek God's guidance for your intercessory prayers. Target the dark places He reveals to you, using your prayers as beams of light to dispel the darkness.

JOURNALING **Prompt**

Reflect on your journey as an intercessor of light. Write about the challenges you've faced while trying to maintain your spiritual light in a world that often seems filled with darkness. How has God's Word served as a lamp to your feet during these times?

～

~

～

_____

_____

_____

_____

_____

_____

_____

_____

_____

_____

_____

_____

_____

_____

_____

_____

_____

_____

_____

CHAPTER 3

INTERCESSORS OF DARKNESS

"Search me, O God, and know my heart; try me, and know my anxieties; and see if there is any wicked way in me, and lead me in the way everlasting." (Psalm 139:23-24, NKJV).

This call for divine examination invites us into a deeper understanding of our own hearts and a commitment to walking in the light of God's truth, ensuring we are not led astray into darkness.

I n exploring the shadows that sometimes envelop our spiritual journey, we find a poignant story that mirrors our struggle against the unseen forces that seek to derail our path. This narrative, rooted in the lesson of **The Parable of the Blind Man**, serves as a stark reminder that we, too, must carry our light not only for our guidance but as a beacon for others. It emphasizes the essence of our mission: to illuminate the darkness with the divine light entrusted to us, a light that, despite our own blindness to the spiritual realm, can guide those around us safely, preventing collisions with the unseen.

As bearers of this light, we are called to **Guard the Lamp of God** within us diligently. Like a city on a hill that cannot be hidden, the divine light shining within us can be dimmed by our sinful actions, leaving us vulnerable to falls. This guarding is not a passive act but a conscious, daily effort to ensure that the light of God in our hearts not only remains lit but shines brightly, cutting through the darkness and guiding both ourselves and those around us to safety.

This brings us to the unsettling reality of **Jezebel's Intercessors Operate in Darkness**, a truth that challenges us to remain vigilant. These intercessors, driven by a spirit of lawlessness, seek to extinguish the light we carry, aiming to darken the hearts of Christ's faithful intercessors. Recognizing this threat is crucial, for it is not just our well-being at stake, but that of the broader community we are called to serve.

My **Aha Moment** revealed the existence of these dark intercessors within the Body of Christ, a revelation not born out of scholarly research but imparted by the Spirit.

This understanding underscores the presence of false intercessors whose intentions are far removed from the will of God, seeking instead to prey on the vulnerabilities and wounds of others for their gain.

These **False Intercessors' Characteristics** are a testament to the subtle ways in which the enemy works, turning those once filled with the light of true intercession towards the shadows. Influenced by hurt, wounds, and the lusts of the flesh, these individuals gradually shift away from their divine calling, becoming tools in Jezebel's hands.

The stark warnings about **The Danger of False Gifts** throughout the New Testament serve as a clarion call for discernment and vigilance. The pervasive nature of these warnings across the scriptures underscores the necessity for us to be grounded in the truth, able to discern the genuine from the counterfeit in all aspects of our spiritual walk.

Inner Vows as Jezebel's Strategy reveal how easily we can become ensnared, with vows made in moments of pain or anger unwittingly inviting demonic influences. These vows, often forgotten, continue to influence our actions and spiritual health, making us vulnerable to manipulation by forces that seek to divert us from our path.

My personal **Encounter with Jezebelic Manipula-**

tion serves as a cautionary tale, illustrating how easily we can be led astray when we are not anchored firmly in our faith and understanding of God's Word. It was a moment of potential turning, a crossroads where the choice to succumb to bitterness and anger could have led me into darkness.

The **Qualities of Dark Intercessors** are marked by deception, a lack of sincerity, and a departure from the genuine heart of intercession. Their prayers, tainted by their allegiance to darkness, become obstacles to the fulfillment of God's will, a stark contrast to the life-giving intercession called for by Scripture.

In facing these challenges, the importance of **Self-Examination and Repentance** cannot be overstated. It is only through regular, honest reflection and the willingness to confront and renounce the darkness within us that we can maintain our course as intercessors of light. This process, guided by the Holy Spirit, is essential for our spiritual integrity and effectiveness in the kingdom of God.

As we navigate the complexities of our calling, let us be ever mindful of the light we carry. Let us guard it zealously, shine it brightly, and use it wisely, knowing that in doing so, we fulfill our role as beacons of hope and guidance in a world that so desperately needs the light of Christ.

. . .

REFLECTIVE QUESTIONS

1. Have you ever experienced a moment when you realized the light within you was dimming? What caused it, and how did you respond?

2. Can you identify any inner vows you might have made in response to hurt or disappointment? How do you think these have influenced your spiritual life?

3. Reflect on the warning signs of false intercession. Have you encountered this in your spiritual community? How did it manifest, and what was the outcome?

4. Considering the dangers of false gifts, how can you cultivate discernment to distinguish true spiritual gifts from false ones?

5. How do personal experiences, like the author's encounter with Jezebelic manipulation, impact your understanding of spiritual warfare and the importance of guarding your heart?

Actionable Steps

- **Cultivate** a Heart of Discernment: Regularly seek the Holy Spirit in prayer for the gift of discernment. This divine insight is crucial for navigating the complexities of spiritual warfare and intercession.
- **Equip** Yourself with Knowledge of God's Word: Deepen your understanding of Scripture to recognize the characteristics of true and false intercession. God's Word is the standard by which all spirits must be tested.
- **Engage** in Regular Self-Examination: Invite the Holy Spirit to search your heart and reveal any areas of darkness, including inner vows or unforgiveness. Repentance and renunciation of these ties are essential for maintaining your position as an intercessor of light.

Journaling Prompt

Reflect on the concept of inner vows and their impact on your spiritual walk. Consider any moments when hurt or disappointment might have led you to make declarations over your life. How can you bring these areas before

God for healing and release, and what steps can you take to ensure your heart remains open to God's light and guidance?

~

~

_____

_____

_____

_____

_____

_____

_____

_____

_____

_____

_____

_____

_____

_____

_____

_____

_____

_____

_____

~

_____

_____

_____

_____

_____

_____

_____

_____

_____

_____

_____

_____

_____

_____

_____

_____

_____

_____

_____

_____

_____

_____

_____

_____

CHAPTER 4
WHY JEZEBEL IS ATTRACTED TO INTERCESSION

Let us remember that our fight is not against flesh and blood but against the rulers, against the authorities, against the powers of this dark world and against the spiritual forces of evil in the heavenly realms.

"Put on the full armor of God, so that you can take your stand against the devil's schemes." - Ephesians 6:11 (NKJV)

I n Chapter 4 of our journey together, we delve deeper into the enigmatic allure Jezebel finds in the sacred act of intercession. Through the experiences shared and the wisdom garnered, it's my hope to illuminate the subtle ways this spirit seeks to infiltrate and manipulate the hearts of those dedicated to prayer.

One of the most striking revelations is **Jezebel's Stealth in Intercession**. The story of Holly serves as a poignant reminder that not all who appear devout in their prayer life are aligned with the heart of God. Holly, with her quiet demeanor and consistent presence, seemed like a beacon of devotion. Yet, beneath the surface, her intentions were far from pure, revealing the critical need for discernment in our spiritual communities.

This brings us to the cautionary tale of the dangers presented by **The Dangers of Credential and Charisma**. Holly's background and apparent dedication masked a deeper, darker agenda. It's a vivid illustration of how easily we can be deceived by outward appearances and the importance of seeking the Holy Spirit's guidance in discerning the spirits that may be at work behind the scenes.

Amy's story underscores the **Control and Manipulation Tactics** often employed by those under Jezebel's influence. Her desire to dominate the prayer meetings and silence potential threats revealed a drive not to uplift the community in prayer but to assert control and divert the group from its true purpose.

Similarly, **The Allure of Position and Power** as illustrated by Maggie's story, exposes another facet of Jezebel's strategy. This craving for leadership and recognition, under the guise of spiritual maturity, is a stark reminder of the necessity for leaders to be healed and whole to prevent them from becoming conduits for Jezebel's agenda.

The narrative also sheds light on **Jezebel's Exploitation of Wounds**. The spirit of Jezebel preys on the vulnerable, using unhealed wounds as gateways to influence and manipulate. This exploitation highlights the urgent need for healing within our communities to close the doors Jezebel seeks to enter through.

Impure Motives and Self-Deception are also tools in Jezebel's arsenal. The individuals influenced by this spirit often believe they are serving God, when in reality, they are advancing Jezebel's destructive purposes. This self-deception is a powerful force, making it challenging to bring those under its sway back to the truth.

Jezebel's Desire for Proximity in prayer circles is not just a matter of physical closeness but a strategic position from which to exert influence and spread her deception more effectively, highlighting the importance of spiritual boundaries within our communities.

The penchant for **False Prophecies and Teachings** among Jezebel's intercessors is a critical area of concern. False prophecies and teachings lead the faithful astray, emphasizing the need for a solid foundation in Scripture and a strong relationship with the Holy Spirit to discern truth from falsehood.

Jezebel's Thirst for Admiration and the **Religious Spirit of Jezebel** further unveil the depth of this spirit's desire not just for control but for recognition and adulation, all while cloaking itself in a facade of piety and devotion. These elements serve as a stark reminder of the constant vigilance required to guard our hearts and communities against the insidious influence of Jezebel.

As we navigate the complexities of spiritual leadership and community, let us hold fast to the wisdom and discernment that comes from a deep, abiding relationship with Christ. In doing so, we can ensure that our gatherings remain places of genuine worship and powerful intercession, free from the influence of Jezebel and her emissaries.

REFLECTIVE QUESTIONS

1. Have you ever encountered an individual in your prayer community whose influence became divisive or harmful? How was this addressed?

2. Reflect on the importance of discerning spirits in leadership and mentorship within prayer

groups. Have you witnessed the consequences
of failing to do so?

3. In what ways can unhealed wounds or desires
for recognition influence one's participation
in intercessory prayer? Have you seen this in
yourself or others?

4. How can communities safeguard against the
influence of Jezebel in their midst, ensuring
that their focus remains on God's will rather
than human agendas?

5. Consider the balance between welcoming
new members into prayer ministries and the
necessity for spiritual discernment. How can
this balance be maintained?

Actionable Steps

- **Cultivate Discernment and Healing**:
Prioritize personal and communal
discernment and healing ministries within
your prayer community to guard against
infiltration by spirits contrary to God's will.

- **Equip with Biblical Knowledge**: Strengthen
your prayer group by deepening your
collective understanding of Scripture,
focusing on teachings about discernment,

spiritual warfare, and the characteristics of true godly leadership.

- **Engage in Transparent Leadership Practices**: Foster an environment where leadership is transparent, accountable, and open to scrutiny under the Word of God, reducing the likelihood of manipulation by those with impure motives.

JOURNALING Prompt

Reflect on your personal experiences within prayer groups or communities. Have you ever felt drawn to a position or recognition more than the act of intercession itself? How can you ensure your heart remains aligned with God's purposes, avoiding the snares of ambition or the influence of a Jezebel spirit?

∿

~

_____

_____

_____

_____

_____

_____

_____

_____

_____

_____

_____

_____

_____

_____

_____

_____

_____

_____

_____

_____

_____

~

_____

_____

_____

_____

_____

_____

_____

_____

_____

_____

_____

_____

_____

_____

_____

_____

_____

_____

_____

_____

_____

CHAPTER 5

WHY JEZEBEL'S INTERCESSORS ARE SO DANGEROUS

This scripture serves as a beacon, guiding us through the complexities of spiritual warfare, illuminating our path as we navigate the treacherous waters stirred by Jezebel's intercessors.

Proverbs 3:5-6 (NKJV) "Trust in the Lord with all your heart, And lean not on your own understanding; In all your ways acknowledge Him, And He shall direct your paths."

As we journey into the heart of this chapter, it's crucial to understand why **Jezebel is a False Prophet in Disguise.** Jezebel's intercessors cleverly conceal their true intentions, masquerading as bearers of divine insight while leading the faithful astray with false prophecies. Their words, though laced with spiritual vernacular, are rooted in deception and aim to sow discord among God's people.

The presence of a **Political Spirit** in these intercessors cannot be overstated. They maneuver through spiritual communities with a hidden agenda, leveraging their influence to create divisions and amass power for themselves. This spirit thrives on competition and seeks to elevate itself by undermining the authority and unity of the church.

One of the most insidious tactics employed by Jezebel's intercessors is the release of **Witchcraft Prayers**. These are prayers that seek to impose one's will over God's divine plan, manipulating circumstances and individuals through spiritual coercion rather than seeking the Lord's guidance and surrendering to His will.

Their mission is clear; they are **On a Seek-and-Destroy Mission**, targeting the very foundation of God's work among His people. By introducing confusion, doubt, and discord, they attempt to dismantle the unity and purpose of the church, hindering the advancement of the Kingdom.

As **Masters of Distraction**, Jezebel's intercessors draw attention away from the core mission of the church, introducing drama and chaos that sap the energy and focus of the faithful. This tactic not only diverts resources but also prevents the body of Christ from pursuing its divine mandate with clarity and unity.

In their quest for dominance, these intercessors also work to **Discredit True Intercessors**, challenging their motives and integrity. By casting shadows of doubt on those genuinely seeking to advance God's kingdom, Jezebel's followers aim to isolate and silence the voices of truth and purity.

Jezebel's desire to **Seek Disciples to Make Spiritual Eunuchs** reveals her ultimate goal: to strip individuals of their spiritual power and autonomy, rendering them ineffective in the battle against darkness. This strategy not only weakens the church's intercessory front but also ensures that these captives are bound to Jezebel's whims.

The **Thriving on Information** aspect of Jezebel's intercessors underscores their hunger for knowledge that can be twisted for manipulative purposes. By gathering intimate details about individuals and ministries, they craft targeted attacks that undermine the work of God.

Their **Desire for Proximity** allows Jezebel's intercessors to exercise influence from within, often going unnoticed until substantial damage has been inflicted. This close access to leaders and the congregation enables them to weave their deceit more effectively.

Finally, the allure of **Being Platformed** speaks to the pride and ambition driving Jezebel's intercessors. They seek visibility and recognition not for the glory of God but to satiate their vanity and to manipulate the narrative within the church to their advantage.

As we journey through this chapter, let us remain vigilant, aware that the dangers posed by Jezebel's intercessors are both real and potent.

> *By equipping ourselves with discernment and a steadfast commitment to God's truth, we can safeguard our communities from the insidious influence of these false prophets.*

REFLECTIVE QUESTIONS

1. Have you encountered individuals in your spiritual community whose actions seemed misaligned with their spiritual declarations? How did you address the situation?
2. Reflect on a time when you felt the influence of manipulative prayers. How did you discern the source and protect yourself?
3. Can you identify a situation where political or divisive spirits attempted to infiltrate your

community? What measures were taken to restore unity and focus?

4. In what ways can we safeguard our ministries and prayer groups from those who seek to discredit true intercessors?

5. How can we foster an environment that discerns and resists the seduction of false doctrine and ensures adherence to biblical truth?

Actionable Steps

- **Cultivate Discernment**: Regularly engage in study and prayer to sharpen your spiritual discernment, enabling you to recognize and resist the influence of Jezebel's intercessors.

- **Equip with Knowledge**: Educate your community on the characteristics and tactics of Jezebel's intercessors, preparing them to stand firm against deception and manipulation.

- **Engage in Spiritual Warfare**: Develop a robust spiritual warfare strategy that includes prayer, fasting, and the application of biblical truths to combat the influence of Jezebel's intercessors effectively.

Journaling Prompt

Reflect on the importance of maintaining purity and integrity in your intercessory practices. Consider any adjustments you might need to make in your spiritual life to ensure you are not inadvertently aligning with the tactics of Jezebel's intercessors. How can you contribute to creating a spiritually healthy and discerning community?

~

~

_____

_____

_____

_____

_____

_____

_____

_____

_____

_____

_____

_____

_____

_____

_____

_____

_____

_____

_____

~

CHAPTER 6
PROTECTION, POWER, AND PRESTIGE

In the journey of intercession, it's vital we stay anchored in truth and humility, recognizing our authority comes from Christ alone. Our defense against the spirit of Jezebel isn't in our strength but in our surrender to God's will, finding our protection under His wings, our power in His Spirit, and our prestige in His calling on our lives. Let's commit to being intercessors who seek God's glory above all, ensuring our prayer life is a reflection of His heart and purposes.

"Beware of false prophets, who come to you in sheep's clothing, but inwardly they are ravenous wolves. You will know them by their fruits. Do men gather grapes from thornbushes or figs from thistles? Even so, every good tree bears good fruit, but a bad

43

tree bears bad fruit. A good tree cannot bear bad fruit, nor can a bad tree bear good fruit. Every tree that does not bear good fruit is cut down and thrown into the fire. Therefore by their fruits you will know them." - Matthew 7:15-20 (NKJV)

As we look deeper into understanding the complex dynamics within prayer communities, it becomes crucial to recognize the subtle yet destructive influence of Jezebel's intercessors. These individuals, driven by a quest for **protection, power, and prestige**, often mask their true intentions under the guise of fervent prayer and devotion. It's essential for leaders and members alike to discern these influences to maintain the purity and integrity of our prayer efforts.

Firstly, the pursuit of **protection** by Jezebel's intercessors reveals a manipulative tactic to gain favor and shield themselves from accountability. Their passionate intercessions, though seemingly sincere, may serve more as a cloak for their underlying motives, creating a false sense of security among leaders and peers. This dynamic can lead to a dangerous blind spot within the community, where the true spiritual health of the group is compromised by the unchecked influence of these intercessors.

Moreover, the **theatrical nature of their prayers**

underscores a troubling trend where the focus shifts from genuine communion with God to a performance designed to draw attention and admiration. This approach not only distracts from the true purpose of prayer but also sows seeds of confusion and division within the group, as members struggle to discern between heartfelt supplication and manipulative theatrics.

The emotional instability displayed by some intercessors, such as sudden bouts of weeping or despair, may indicate deeper spiritual struggles or alignments with Jezebel's manipulative spirit. Recognizing these signs is crucial for providing appropriate support and guidance, ensuring that prayer remains a source of healing and empowerment, rather than a platform for personal turmoil.

Jezebel's intercessors often crave a **commanding position** within the prayer community, not merely for the sake of service but for the esteem and influence it affords. This desire for prestige can lead to manipulative behaviors, as individuals seek to position themselves as spiritual elites, undermining the collective focus on God's will.

The **Jekyll and Hyde persona** is a stark reminder of the duplicity that can exist within prayer groups, where an intercessor's public displays of piety mask a darker, self-serving agenda. Leaders must exercise discernment to navigate these complex dynamics, ensuring that the prayer community remains a space for genuine spiritual growth.

The relentless pursuit of **power** mirrors the biblical narrative of Lucifer's fall, highlighting the dangers of unchecked ambition within spiritual communities. Jezebel's intercessors, dissatisfied with serving under authority, seek to usurp or undermine leadership to fulfill their own ambitions, threatening the unity and mission of the group.

When faced with **correction**, Jezebel's intercessors often react with defensiveness or blame-shifting, indicating a refusal to acknowledge wrongdoing or align with the community's values. This resistance to accountability is a red flag, signaling deeper issues of rebellion and alignment with Jezebel's spirit.

Attention-seeking behavior among Jezebel's intercessors further complicates the community's dynamics, as individuals engage in exaggerated displays of spirituality to garner praise and recognition. This self-exaltation not only distracts from the communal focus on God but also erodes the integrity of the prayer effort.

The tendency to prophesy, even when not Spirit-led, demonstrates Jezebel's intercessors' desire to influence and manipulate the group's direction. Discerning the source and intent of prophetic utterances is essential for safeguarding the community's spiritual health.

Finally, Jezebel's intercessors' inability to accept **correction** without becoming defensive or combative underscores the importance of fostering a culture of humility and mutual accountability within prayer communities. Leaders must navigate these challenges with wisdom and grace, ensuring that the prayer group remains anchored in truth and unity.

In addressing these challenges, we must remember that our struggle is not against flesh and blood but against spiritual forces seeking to disrupt and divide. By cultivating discernment, fostering genuine fellowship, and maintaining a steadfast focus on God's will, we can protect our prayer communities from the influence of Jezebel's intercessors and continue to advance the Kingdom of God with integrity and power.

REFLECTIVE QUESTIONS

1. **How can we cultivate discernment** to recognize the subtle influences of Jezebel's intercessors within our prayer communities?

2. **What strategies can we implement to ensure our prayer groups are protected**

from the divisive tactics of Jezebel's intercessors?

3. **In what ways can we foster an environment of accountability and transparency** to mitigate the impact of those seeking power and prestige through manipulation?

4. **How can we respond with grace and wisdom when confronted with emotional instability** or theatrical displays of spirituality that may hint at deeper issues?

5. **What measures can be taken to preserve unity and integrity within our prayer communities**, especially when faced with attempts to divide and conquer?

Actionable Steps

- **Cultivate** a culture of humility and servanthood within your prayer community to counteract the allure of power and prestige.
- **Equip** members of your prayer community with teachings on spiritual discernment and the characteristics of a pure heart, to recognize and resist Jezebel's influence.

- **Engage** in regular prayer and fasting for the protection of your prayer community, asking God to reveal hidden motives and to strengthen the bonds of unity and love among members.

Journaling Prompt

Reflect on any encounters or experiences within your prayer community that may have been influenced by the spirit of Jezebel. How did you respond, and what lessons did you learn? Consider how you can apply these insights to strengthen your spiritual discernment and protect your community from similar challenges in the future.

~

~

~

_____

_____

_____

_____

_____

_____

_____

_____

_____

_____

_____

_____

_____

_____

_____

_____

_____

_____

CHAPTER 7

PROPHESYING, TEACHING, UNDERMINING, AND DOMINATING

Stay vigilant and grounded in God's Word, for our strength and discernment come from Him. Let us pray without ceasing, not for our glory but for His kingdom to be revealed on earth. Remember,

"For God is not the author of confusion but of peace, as in all the churches of the saints." (1 Corinthians 14:33, NKJV).

As we look into the realm of spiritual warfare and intercession, it's vital to recognize the subtleties of the Jezebel spirit, especially when it manifests in prayer groups. This spirit, known for its manipulative and destructive tendencies, often reveals itself through specific behaviors and actions that can undermine the very core of our spiritual communities. Let's explore these manifestations further to equip ourselves with the knowledge and discernment needed to stand firm in our faith and protect the sanctity of our prayer groups.

Jezebel Loves to Prophesy, but not with the purity and truth of the Holy Spirit. Instead, this spirit uses prophecy as a tool for manipulation, drawing attention and allegiance away from God. This counterfeit prophecy may appear accurate, yet it's driven by a desire for control and personal gain, leading many astray with its seductive allure.

Another tactic is how **Jezebel Loves to Teach**, twisting Scripture to fit a nefarious agenda. This false teaching, often disguised as deep spiritual insight, directly undermines the leadership and teachings of the church, spreading heresy and confusion among the faithful.

In prayer meetings, the Jezebel spirit will attempt to **Dominate the Prayer Flow**, asserting its agenda over the collective will of the group. This domination disrupts the unity and direction of prayer, steering the focus away from God's will and towards its destructive purposes.

Criticism is another weapon in Jezebel's arsenal.

Jezebel the Critic finds fault in others' prayers and actions, using criticism to elevate itself while diminishing the contributions and spirituality of others. This critical spirit, rooted in pride and insecurity, seeks to divide and conquer, sowing seeds of discord within the community.

Jezebel's intercessors work to **Undermine Leadership Authority**, presenting themselves as allies while covertly challenging and subverting the established spiritual authority. This undermining is a strategic move to gain power and influence, positioning the Jezebel spirit as an alternate source of guidance and authority.

By **Creating Soul Ties** with individuals within the prayer group, Jezebel's intercessors forge unhealthy emotional bonds that manipulate and maintain their influence. These soul ties, reminiscent of the bond between Jezebel and Ahab, draw individuals away from godly relationships and accountability, making it difficult to resist their influence.

Character Assassination is a sinister tactic used by Jezebel's intercessors to attack and discredit those who stand in their way. Through lies and exaggerations, they aim to destroy reputations, leveraging the power of false accusations to eliminate threats to their control.

Jezebel's intercessors are both **Offensive and Easily Offended**, reacting aggressively to righteousness and correction. Their inability to accept denial or critique without taking offense reveals their lack of submission to godly authority and their opposition to the truth.

Driven by envy, **Jezebel is Jealous and Competitive**, seeking to outshine others in spiritual displays not for the glory of God but for personal recognition. This competitive spirit is antithetical to the cooperative and humble nature of genuine intercession, where the focus should be on God's will rather than human accolades.

Lastly, Jezebel's intercessors engage in **Public Displays for Attention**, performing actions that draw eyes to themselves rather than directing hearts towards God. These attention-seeking stunts are designed to gain admiration and influence, furthering their agenda at the expense of true spiritual engagement.

By understanding these ten key points, we can better identify and address the presence of the Jezebel spirit within our prayer groups. It's through this discernment, grounded in Scripture and prayer, that we can protect our communities from the insidious influence of Jezebel's intercessors, ensuring our collective focus remains steadfastly on God.

~

1. Have you ever encountered someone in your prayer group who seemed more focused on drawing attention to themselves than on seeking God's will?
2. How can we discern between genuine prophecy led by the Holy Spirit and prophetic witchcraft influenced by a Jezebel spirit?
3. In what ways can we protect our prayer groups from individuals who seek to dominate or derail the prayer flow?
4. What steps can we take to ensure criticism within our prayer communities is constructive and aligned with God's word, rather than destructive and divisive?
5. How can we maintain a posture of humility and openness to correction, ensuring we do not fall into the traps set by a Jezebel spirit?

Actionable Steps

- **Cultivate a Culture of Discernment:** Encourage regular teachings on discernment and the characteristics of a Jezebel spirit within your prayer group to equip members to recognize and resist such influences.

- **Equip with Scriptural Understanding**: Provide comprehensive Bible study sessions focused on the nature of true prophecy, godly teaching, and the importance of submission to godly authority, to build a solid scriptural foundation among intercessors.

- **Engage in Fervent Prayer for Protection**: Regularly include prayers for protection against the influence of the Jezebel spirit in your prayer meetings, asking for unity, purity, and discernment for all members.

JOURNALING Prompt

Reflect on a time when you felt the dynamics of your prayer group were being influenced by someone's personal agenda rather than the Holy Spirit. What were the signs, and how was the situation resolved? How did it deepen your understanding of the need for discernment and unity in prayer?

~

～

_____

_____

_____

_____

_____

_____

_____

_____

_____

_____

_____

_____

_____

_____

_____

_____

_____

_____

_____

_____

~

_____

_____

_____

_____

_____

_____

_____

_____

_____

_____

_____

_____

_____

_____

_____

_____

_____

_____

_____

_____

CHAPTER 8

GROOMING SONS, SPIES, MESSENGERS, AND FALSE PROPHETS

Let us hold fast to the wisdom that is from above, which is first pure, then peaceable, gentle, willing to yield, full of mercy and good fruits, without partiality and without hypocrisy. As we stand firm in our faith, let us also extend grace, knowing that those entangled in Jezebel's web are in need of deliverance and the love of Christ.

"Submit yourselves therefore to God. Resist the devil, and he will flee from you." - James 4:7 (NKJV)

One of the most pernicious tactics employed by Jezebel's intercessors is the **birthing of spiritual sons and daughters.** Through manipulative mentorship, these individuals replicate their deceptive practices, creating a lineage that perpetuates their agenda. By drawing vulnerable believers into their fold, they aim to expand their sphere of influence, sowing seeds of division and confusion.

Deploying spies within spiritual communities allows Jezebel's intercessors to gather intelligence, leveraging this information to manipulate situations and individuals to their advantage. These spies, acting under the guise of concern and fellowship, seek out weaknesses and vulnerabilities, weaponizing what they learn against the community.

The **dispatch of messengers** to carry out their schemes is another hallmark of their operation. These messengers, often unaware of the full extent of their role, spread misinformation and discord, undermining the leadership and sowing seeds of doubt among the faithful.

Through **strong intimidation and spiritual abuse**, Jezebel's intercessors exert control over others. This abuse, both overt and subtle, seeks to coerce submission to their will, leaving individuals feeling isolated, confused, and spiritually depleted.

The **seduction of false prophets** is a particularly dangerous aspect of Jezebel's influence. By masquerading as gifted prophets, these intercessors lure seekers away from true spiritual paths, offering false assurances and prophecies that lead only to disillusionment and despair.

A relentless pursuit of visibility and influence drives

Jezebel's intercessors to **covet platforms** within spiritual communities. They seek not to serve, but to be seen, using others' platforms as stepping stones to elevate their status and spread their corrupt teachings.

Curses and judgment, wielded as weapons, are used to intimidate and harm those who stand in opposition to Jezebel's aims. These curses, often cloaked in spiritual language, are designed to instill fear and compliance.

Their behavior is characterized by being both **offensive and easily offended**. Quick to take umbrage at perceived slights, they use their offense as a weapon, manipulating situations to their advantage while deflecting any criticism of their actions.

A **jealous and competitive** nature underpins their interactions within the community. Unable to rejoice in the successes of others, they view every achievement as a threat to their quest for dominance and recognition.

Finally, the **undermining of leadership authority** is a critical strategy in Jezebel's playbook. By challenging the legitimacy and guidance of spiritual leaders, these intercessors seek to destabilize the foundation of the community, hoping to insert themselves into positions of power and influence.

As we journey together through this study, let us be mindful of these strategies, cultivating a spirit of discernment that allows us to recognize and resist the influence of Jezebel's intercessors. In doing so, we safeguard the integrity of our communities, ensuring that they remain places of growth, healing, and genuine spiritual fellowship.

REFLECTIVE QUESTIONS

1. **How can we cultivate discernment** to recognize the subtle influences of Jezebel's intercessors in our communities?
2. **What steps can we take to protect our spiritual family** from the divisive tactics of Jezebel's intercessors?
3. **In what ways might we unintentionally give platform or influence** to those operating under Jezebel's spirit, and how can we rectify this?
4. **How can we ensure that our desire for spiritual gifts and guidance** does not make us susceptible to the seductions of false prophets?
5. **What measures can we implement to foster an environment** where truth and love prevail over manipulation and control?

Actionable Steps

- **Cultivate a Spirit of Discernment:** Regularly seek the wisdom and guidance of the Holy Spirit through prayer and the study of Scripture to recognize the workings of deceptive spirits.
- **Equip the Community with Knowledge:** Offer teachings and workshops on spiritual warfare and discernment to empower individuals to recognize and resist manipulative tactics.
- **Engage in Regular Spiritual Accountability:** Foster a culture of openness and accountability within leadership and among members to guard against the influence of divisive spirits.

Journaling Prompt

Reflect on any experiences or encounters you have had with individuals who may have been operating under Jezebel's influence. How did it affect you and your community? What steps did you take, or could you have taken, to address the situation? How can you apply the lessons learned from these experiences to better protect and nurture your spiritual environment?

~

~

_____

_____

_____

_____

_____

_____

_____

_____

_____

_____

_____

_____

_____

_____

_____

_____

_____

_____

~

_____

_____

_____

_____

_____

_____

_____

_____

_____

_____

_____

_____

_____

_____

_____

_____

_____

_____

_____

_____

_____

_____

CHAPTER 9
AVOIDING TAPPING INTO WITCHCRAFT PRAYERS

In your walk with God, it's paramount to ensure that your prayers are aligned with His will, not tainted by personal desires that oppose His divine plans. Through my journey, I've learned that prayer, at its core, should be a reflection of our submission and trust in God's sovereignty. Let me share an encouragement that has been a beacon for me: Let your prayers be the echo of God's voice, not the shadow of your desires. This truth underscores the essence of prayer as a communion with God, where His will takes precedence over our wants.

"For this is the confidence that we have in Him, that if we ask anything according to His will, He hears us." - 1 John 5:14 (NKJV)

A s we journey deeper into understanding the spiritual dynamics that influence our prayer life, it becomes evident that not all prayers ascend to the throne of grace in the manner we might expect. In my experience, I've come to recognize a subtle yet profound distinction in the nature of our prayers, especially when influenced by the spirit of Jezebel. This influence can lead us into a realm I refer to as **witchcraft prayers**, which are not led by the Spirit. These prayers, often well-intentioned, seek to impose our will over God's, contrary to the submissive posture we're called to embrace in our communication with the Father.

It's an uncomfortable truth that **Jezebel's intercessors can pray witchcraft prayers unknowingly.** Their prayers, emanating from a place of hurt or a desire for control, may not overtly intend to oppose God's will. Yet, the essence of these prayers does precisely that by elevating our desires above His sovereign plans. This brings us to a critical understanding of **the nature of witchcraft prayers.** These prayers range from benign to malignant, with some simply falling flat, while others actively invite harm or manipulation into someone's life or circumstances.

In a Christian context, identifying witchcraft prayers requires discernment. These prayers often manifest as attempts to control situations or people rather than surrendering to God's sovereignty. This is where the **goal of Jezebel's witchcraft prayers** becomes clear: to assert control, manipulate situations or individuals, and deviate from submission to God's will. The **danger of these prayers** is profound, as they can open doors for the enemy to work against us or those for whom we pray, causing confusion, harm, and spiritual bondage.

God's stance on witchcraft is unequivocal. It is condemned and considered rebellious and hostile towards Him, as it seeks to elevate our desires above His plans. T

> *his understanding compels us to avoid witch-craft prayers by aligning with God's will, ensuring our prayers are rooted in love, faith, and submission to His will, rather than our own.*

One might wonder about the impact of witchcraft prayers on the one praying. Such prayers can lead to spiritual blindness, where the intercessor cannot discern God's voice, leading to a deeper entanglement with Jezebel's influence. It's a sobering thought that prompts a reflection on our heart motives and the purity of our prayers.

Moreover, the **solution and protection against witchcraft prayers** lie in cultivating a heart of humility, seeking God's will above our own, and staying grounded in Scripture. This approach safeguards our prayers from witchcraft, ensuring they ascend as a sweet incense to the Lord, rooted in humility and submission to His perfect will.

As we navigate our prayer life, let us be vigilant against the subtle infiltration of witchcraft prayers. Let us commit to **checking our heart motives**, ensuring they align with the Spirit of God, and embrace a posture of submission and love in our prayers. By doing so, we protect not only our spiritual well-being but also contribute to the edification of the Body of Christ, standing as faithful intercessors whose prayers are pleasing to the Lord.

REFLECTIVE QUESTIONS

1. Have you ever found yourself praying for your will to be done instead of seeking God's will? How can you redirect such prayers?
2. Reflect on a time when you might have prayed out of hurt or desire for control. How can you

ensure your prayers are Spirit-led moving forward?

3. How can you guard your heart against the influence of Jezebel in your intercessory prayer life?

4. In what ways can you cultivate a deeper submission to God's will in your prayer life?

5. How can recognizing the nature of witchcraft prayers impact your approach to intercession?

Actionable Steps

- **Cultivate a Heart of Submission**: Regularly meditate on Scriptures that emphasize God's sovereignty and our call to submit to His will in prayer.

- **Equip Yourself with Discernment**: Engage in studies and teachings on discernment to better identify when prayers may be crossing into manipulation or control.

- **Engage in Accountability**: Share your prayer requests with a trusted spiritual mentor or prayer group that can help ensure your prayers align with God's will.

JOURNALING Prompt

Reflect on the concept of witchcraft prayers and how they contrast with prayers led by the Holy Spirit. Consider how you can more deeply align your prayer life with God's will and the steps you need to take to avoid inadvertently tapping into witchcraft.

~

_____

_____

_____

_____

_____

_____

_____

_____

_____

_____

_____

_____

_____

_____

_____

_____

_____

_____

_____

_____

CHAPTER 10

CONFRONTING JEZEBEL'S INTERCESSORS

Remember, confronting the spirit of Jezebel is not just a battle but a mandate for every believer who desires to see the purity and unity of the Body of Christ maintained. It requires courage, wisdom, and reliance on the Holy Spirit. The Lord is with you, equipping and empowering you for every good work.

James 4:7 NKJV "Therefore submit to God. Resist the devil and he will flee from you."

In Chapter 10, we journey into a critical aspect of spiritual leadership and discernment, confronting the Jezebel spirit's intercessors. This chapter is not just a narrative but a guide, drawing from a painful yet enlightening experience in our ministry. The **Necessity**

of Timely Intervention becomes clear as we reflect on a situation that was allowed to escalate far beyond what was manageable. Looking back, the intervention was long overdue. The wounds inflicted by Jezebel's influence were deep, causing not just spiritual but emotional turmoil within our congregation. This realization hit hard; had we acted sooner, much of the pain could have been mitigated.

As we look deeper into the dynamics within our congregation, it becomes evident that appearances can be deceiving. This brings us to our second key point, the **Recognition of Disguised Harm**. A member of our community, whom we'll refer to as Earlene, exemplified this. On the surface, Earlene was the epitome of a devoted churchgoer, always ready to lend a hand. However, her actions belied a deeper, more insidious motive. She overstepped her bounds, assuming authority that was never hers to take. This situation underscores the importance of vigilance and discernment in recognizing those who, under the guise of helpfulness, seek to sow discord and manipulate others for their gain.

This leads us into understanding the **Importance of Spiritual Authority**. Earlene's actions were a classic example of how the Jezebel spirit operates by undermining established spiritual authority within the church. It was a stark reminder that spiritual boundaries are set for a reason, and when these are crossed, it opens the door to chaos and division. Upholding and respecting these boundaries is crucial for the health and unity of the church body.

Our ordeal with Earlene also shed light on the **Dangers of Covert Operations**. Her strategy was to operate under the radar, presenting herself as a beacon of volunteerism while secretly drawing vulnerable members of the congregation into her web. This deception was particularly insidious because it was hidden under a veneer of righteousness, making it all the more difficult to confront.

The situation with Earlene reached a tipping point, emphasizing the **Power of Unity in Leadership**. It was only through a united front that we were able to address the issue effectively. Our collective decision to confront Earlene was not made lightly, but it was necessary for the health of our church community. This unity among the leadership was a testament to the strength that comes from a shared commitment to truth and righteousness.

Addressing the situation required more than just a willingness to confront; it required a divinely inspired **Discernment and Strategy**. Our approach to dealing with Earlene was prayerfully considered, guided by the Holy Spirit. This strategic, discerning approach underscored the complexity of confronting such deeply ingrained spiritual issues.

The actual **Process of Confrontation** was one of the most challenging aspects of this journey.

> *It was a delicate balance between speaking the truth in love and maintaining a firm stance against the behaviors that were causing so much damage within our church.*

This process was not about personal vendettas but about seeking restoration and healing for all involved, including Earlene.

In the aftermath of the confrontation, we witnessed the transformative power of taking decisive action. The **Outcome of Confrontation** was a testament to the fact that, while difficult, such actions are often necessary for the greater good. Our church experienced a renewal, marked by growth and a deeper sense of community. This outcome served as a powerful reminder of the positive changes that can come from confronting difficult truths.

For some, the confrontation with a Jezebelic influence may not be direct but may instead involve a personal decision to leave a toxic environment. This brings us to the understanding that sometimes **The Choice to Leave or Stay** is the most effective form of confrontation. In situations where the Jezebel spirit is allowed free reign, removing oneself from its influence can be an act of spiritual preservation and integrity.

Lastly, through all these experiences, the **Importance of Personal Holiness** has been a recurring theme. It's a reminder that confronting the spirit of Jezebel

begins with a heart that seeks after God, one that is pure and submitted to His will.

This personal holiness is what empowers us to stand against the deception and manipulation of the Jezebel spirit, equipped with the full armor of God.

In closing, Chapter 10 is not just a recounting of a difficult period in our ministry; it's a call to vigilance, discernment, and spiritual courage. It's a reminder that the spirit of Jezebel is a real and present danger in many congregations today, but with the right approach and reliance on God, it can be confronted and overcome. Let us walk in unity, discernment, and holiness, always ready to protect the integrity of our faith communities.

Reflective Questions

1. Have I ever witnessed or experienced the influence of a Jezebelic spirit within my church or community? What were the signs?
2. In what ways can I cultivate discernment to recognize the subtle operations of a Jezebelic spirit?
3. How does the concept of spiritual authority play out in my life and church? Am I respecting and upholding the boundaries set by my leaders?
4. What steps can I take to ensure unity among church leadership to stand strong against divisive spirits?
5. How can I prepare myself spiritually and mentally for the possibility of confronting or dealing with a Jezebelic influence?

Actionable Steps

- **Cultivate** a Discerning Spirit: Spend time in prayer and God's Word to sharpen your spiritual discernment, enabling you to recognize and understand the subtle workings of Jezebel's spirit.

- **Equip** Yourself with Knowledge: Learn about the characteristics of the Jezebel spirit and the biblical way to confront it. Equip yourself with the armor of God (Ephesians 6:10-18) to stand firm against spiritual warfare.

- **Engage** in Spiritual Warfare and Intercession: Actively pray against the influence of the Jezebel spirit in your community, and intercede for those who may be under its sway. Seek the Lord for strategies to deal with this spirit effectively.

Journaling Prompt

Reflect on a time when you had to make a difficult decision to confront something harmful or leave a harmful situation for the sake of righteousness. How did you see God's hand in guiding and protecting you through that process?

~

~

_____

_____

_____

_____

_____

_____

_____

_____

_____

_____

_____

_____

_____

_____

_____

_____

_____

_____

_____

_____

~

_____

_____

_____

_____

_____

_____

_____

_____

_____

_____

_____

_____

_____

_____

_____

_____

_____

_____

_____

_____

_____

_____

DEALING WITH JEZEBEL'S AFTERMATH

Romans 8:37 NKJV: "Yet in all these things we are more than conquerors through Him who loved us."

No aftermath is too great for God's healing and restoration.

In reflecting upon the challenges we face after confronting the spirit of Jezebel, it's crucial to understand that the battle does not end with the confrontation. The **Inevitability of Aftermath** serves as a stark reminder that our spiritual engagements often leave a lingering impact, much like the devastation witnessed in the historical events of Hiroshima and Nagasaki. This aftermath can deeply affect our communities, necessitating a period of healing and reconstruction.

Recognizing this inevitability is the first step toward navigating the path to recovery.

The aftermath of Jezebel's influence isn't confined to the immediate fallout; rather, it unfolds over time. The **Duration of Ripple Effects** can extend for months, revealing the depth of Jezebel's impact on individuals and the community. This protracted period of discovery and healing underscores the need for patience and continued vigilance. As leaders and believers, our response to these revelations shapes the healing process and the restoration of trust within our community.

Maintaining **The Importance of Alertness** is critical in this period of vulnerability. Like a lion hunting its prey, the spirit of Jezebel, or its affiliates like Athaliah, waits for moments of weakness or distraction to strike. This emphasizes the need for constant vigilance, not out of fear, but from a place of spiritual readiness, ensuring we are prepared for any subsequent attacks or challenges that may arise.

In the wake of Jezebel's influence, we might encounter **The Significance of Discernment in Identifying Athaliah**. Athaliah, representing a new but related threat, can emerge, requiring a distinct approach to confront and overcome. This period calls for discernment to differentiate between the spirits at work and to apply the correct spiritual strategies. Understanding the nuances between these spirits is essential for effectively addressing the unique challenges they present.

During these times, **The Power of Encouragement in the Lord** becomes our refuge and strength.

Just as David found strength in God amidst his own battles, we too must turn to Him for encouragement and renewal.

This divine strength is not just a source of personal fortitude but also a beacon of hope for our communities, reminding us that no aftermath is too great for God's healing touch.

The Strategy of Rallying the Troops is a pivotal action in our recovery efforts. Mobilizing a united front for spiritual warfare and intercession helps to close any open doors left in Jezebel's wake and to uproot any lingering influences. This collective effort not only fortifies our spiritual defenses but also fosters a sense of unity and purpose among the believers, reinforcing the communal bonds that Jezebel sought to sever.

As we rebuild, **The Necessity of Strengthening What Remains** becomes apparent. This involves not just repairing the visible damage but also reinforcing the spiritual health and resilience of our community. Establishing stronger protocols and fostering an environment of spiritual growth and accountability helps prevent future infiltrations and ensures that our community is built on a firm foundation of faith.

In the aftermath of such spiritual battles, there's a real danger of becoming guarded and withdrawn. However, **The Danger of Closing Your Heart** serves as a caution against this response.

An open heart is essential for healing, ministry, and moving forward in God's grace. It's through our openness that we can extend forgiveness, foster healing, and continue to serve effectively in our calling.

Post-conflict, **The Importance of Debriefing After Battle** offers us a chance to reflect, learn, and prepare for the future. This process of debriefing allows us to dissect the events, understand the enemy's tactics, and recognize God's hand in our victory. Through this reflective practice, we can glean valuable insights that will equip us for future engagements with the enemy.

Lastly, it's essential to exercise caution and seek divine guidance to avoid **The Caution Against False Jezebel Accusations.** Mislabeling individuals as operating under a Jezebel spirit can cause harm and division, undermining the unity and healing process within our community.

> *By approaching each situation with prayerful consideration and discernment, we can avoid the pitfalls of false accusations and foster a spirit of grace and understanding.*

As we navigate the aftermath of confronting Jezebel, these principles guide us toward recovery, restoration, and renewed strength in our faith communities. Through vigilance, discernment, encouragement, and unity, we can overcome the challenges posed by Jezebel's influence and emerge stronger, both individually and collectively.

REFLECTIVE QUESTIONS

1. How have I experienced the aftermath of spiritual warfare in my own life or community, and what were its long-term effects?

2. In what ways can I cultivate a state of constant vigilance without falling into paranoia?

3. How can I improve my discernment between different spirits, such as Jezebel and Athaliah?

4. What steps can I take to strengthen my spiritual foundation and that of my community to withstand future attacks?

5. How can I maintain an open heart towards others, even after experiencing betrayal or hurt?

Actionable Steps

- **Cultivate an Atmosphere of Vigilance:** Regularly engage in prayer and fellowship to maintain spiritual awareness and readiness against Jezebel's aftermath and any emerging threats.

- **Equip Yourself and Your Community:** Educate yourself and those around you about the tactics of Jezebel and Athaliah, fostering a culture of wisdom and discernment in spiritual warfare.

- **Engage in Strategic Spiritual Warfare:** Organize focused prayer sessions and teachings to address and uproot any lingering or new influences of Jezebel within your community.

Journaling Prompt

Reflect on a time when you had to deal with the aftermath of a spiritual battle. How did you find strength in the Lord during this time? What lessons did you learn, and how have they equipped you for future challenges?

~

~

_____

_____

_____

_____

_____

_____

_____

_____

_____

_____

_____

_____

_____

_____

_____

_____

_____

_____

_____

_____

～

_____

_____

_____

_____

_____

_____

_____

_____

_____

_____

_____

_____

_____

_____

_____

_____

_____

_____

_____

_____

_____

_____

CHAPTER 12
WHAT JEZEBEL'S INTERCESSORS DON'T WANT YOU TO KNOW

"He who is in you is greater than he who is in the world" (1 John 4:4 NKJV).

This promise assures us of victory over Jezebel's schemes.

In my journey through Christianity and particularly through the experiences at my church in South Florida, I have encountered the spirit of Jezebel in ways that have both challenged and deepened my understanding of spiritual warfare. I do not claim to be an expert on the Jezebel spirit or its intercessors, but through the battles faced and the lessons learned, I've come to recognize the truths about this spirit that it desperately does not want us to know.

One of the most crucial insights I've gained is the

Understanding the True Nature of Jezebel. This spirit is far more than just about control or manipulation; it's fundamentally a spirit of seduction, aiming to lead believers away from the path of righteousness and into sin. This revelation underscores the importance of recognizing Jezebel's real goal, which is to seduce God's people into abandoning their faith and embracing sin.

In exploring the **The Significance of Names in Scripture**, I learned that names like Jezebel carry deep meanings and hint at the characteristics of the spirits they represent. Delving into the biblical and historical context of Jezebel's name, which suggests a lack of cohabitation and an unwillingness to share power, opened my eyes to the solitary and dominating nature of this spirit. This understanding is vital for recognizing the operations of Jezebel in a spiritual context.

The historical backdrop of Jezebel, explored through **The Historical and Spiritual Lineage of Jezebel**, reveals its longstanding opposition to God's plans and people. From the Old Testament to the New, Jezebel's spirit has manifested to seduce and mislead, demonstrating the need for vigilance against this ancient foe.

Jezebel's particular animosity towards **Prophets and Intercessors** is a testament to the power and threat that these individuals pose to her agenda. As carriers of God's voice and warriors in prayer, prophets and intercessors are prime targets for Jezebel's attacks, highlighting the need for these servants to be covered in prayer and protected by their communities.

A question that often arises is **Can a Christian have a Jezebel spirit?** Through my experiences, I've come to understand that while Christians cannot be possessed by Jezebel, they can fall under its influence if they provide it with a stronghold through unrepentant sin or unresolved wounds. This insight is crucial for maintaining spiritual health and guarding against deception.

In today's world, the prevalence of Jezebel is unmistakable, which leads to the question, **Do you see the spirit of Jezebel rising in this hour?** Yes, its manifestations in the church and society signal a call to arms for believers to stand firm in their faith and combat this spirit with truth and righteousness.

Understanding **Jezebel's Ultimate Agenda** is key to combating her effectively. Beyond seeking control, Jezebel seeks to destroy individuals' faith through idolatry and immorality. This understanding equips us to recognize and resist her broader strategies of seduction.

Recognizing **Jezebel's Influence in the Church** involves discerning patterns of unchecked sin and the idolization of leaders, which are indicative of her workings. This discernment is vital for maintaining the spiritual health of our congregations.

Preventative and Proactive Measures Against Jezebel involve spiritual vigilance and the application of biblical authority to keep her at bay. Protecting our spiritual territory through prayer and adherence to God's Word is essential for preventing her influence in our lives and communities.

Lastly, **Deliverance from Jezebel Involves Healing and Repentance.** True freedom from this spirit's influence requires addressing the root issues that gave it access, including healing from wounds and repenting from sins.

As we navigate our spiritual journey, these insights into the workings of Jezebel and her intercessors arm us with the knowledge and strategies needed to confront and overcome her deceitful tactics.

By staying rooted in God's Word, covered in prayer, and united in our fight against darkness, we can emerge victorious in our battles against the spirit of Jezebel.

Reflective Questions

1. How can I better understand and identify the spirit of Jezebel in my environment?

2. In what ways can I strengthen my or my community's spiritual defenses against Jezebel's influence?

3. What steps can I take to ensure I am not unknowingly giving Jezebel a foothold in my life?

4. How can I support prophets and intercessors in my community who may be under attack by Jezebel?

5. What healing or repentance do I need to pursue to safeguard myself from Jezebel's seduction?

Actionable Steps

- **Cultivate a Deep Understanding of God's Word**: Regular study and meditation on Scripture arm you with the truth to counter Jezebel's lies and seductions.

- **Equip Yourself with Discernment**: Pray for the gift of discernment to recognize the subtle workings of Jezebel's spirit in your life and in your community.

- **Engage in Fervent Prayer and Intercession**: Commit to regular prayer and intercession, specifically against the spirit of Jezebel, to protect yourself and your community from its influence.

Journaling Prompt

Reflect on any personal encounters you've had with the spirit of Jezebel, either directly or indirectly. How did these experiences challenge your faith, and what did you learn about God's provision and protection during these times?

～

_____

_____

_____

_____

_____

_____

_____

_____

_____

_____

_____

_____

_____

_____

_____

_____

_____

_____

_____

_____

_____

~

Faith and Flame Press is a Christian book publishing company that is passionate about igniting the flames of faith in the hearts of readers around the world. Our mission is to publish books that inspire, enlighten, and uplift the spirit, and help readers deepen their understanding of their faith and spirituality.

At Faith and Flame Press, we believe that books have the power to transform lives and to shape the world we live in. That's why we are committed to publishing books that are not only spiritually uplifting but also intellectually stimulating, well-researched, and thought-provoking.

www.ingramcontent.com/pod-product-compliance
Lightning Source LLC
Chambersburg PA
CBHW070123100426
42744CB00010B/1908